The World, I Guess

The World, I Guess

poems

George Bowering

2015
New Star Books
Vancouver

Published by
New Star Books Ltd.

CANADA
No. 107 -- 3477 Commercial St.
Vancouver, BC   V5N 4E8

USA
No. 1517 -- 1574 Gulf Rd.
Point Roberts, WA 98281

www.NewStarBooks.com
info@NewStarBooks.com

The publisher acknowledges the financial support of the Canada Council for the
Arts, the Government of Canada through the Canada Book Fund, the British
Columbia Arts Council, and the Government of British Columbia through the
Book Publishing Tax Credit.

Cataloguing information is available from Library and Archives Canada, www.
collectionscanada.gc.ca/

Cover design by Oliver McPartlin
Printed on 100 percent post-consumer recycled paper
Printed and bound in Canada by Imprimerie Gauvin, Gatineau, QC.
First printing May 2015

Contents

This collection is for my first reader,
manager, publicist, agent and
sweetheart, Jean L. Baird

Introduction

Early in the second decade of the twenty-first century, Toronto's Ryerson University asked me to come and say something to some of their literature people, students and teachers. So I sat down and started writing something about whatever it was that made me become a writer, particularly a poet. The way things were going now that I was an old hand, I found myself writing little narratives about moments in my early life that took me past the boundary line of comfort into a psyche-region that required not so much words as a realization that something like organized alarm was called for.

I kept going till I had six of these stories. I was thinking of writing ten of them, but ran out of steam after six, and when I got to Ryerson I had time to read only two. Then when it came time to arrange a new volume of poetry, I decided to include a few little tales about the beginnings of this peculiar occupation.

***

There's a truth about the writing life here somewhere.

The World, I Guess

If you don't write it down, the poem will go away,
back to wherever it came from, maybe a dead person
or Mars. Even if you're doing something else, like trying
to have a bowel movement, as is often the case with me,
not meaning to be vulgar or comical, but
a planetoid is another possibility, if that's the right word.

Think about all the poor mute Miltons who had something
else to do; they could have changed the world,
or at least the poetry world, or North America. But
even if you write it down, here's the problem, you will be
mis-writing, because you are mis-reading. You have to accept that
if you want to spend a life at this job.

Reluctant to Talk

What if God keeps picking people to be saviors
and they don't pick up on it? What if
every time He sits down he accidentally squashes
a couple of his sons? The world turns, a big ball
as in all the space movies, and you wonder
which way is east, and don't we usually think
God is over that way? An old truck comes to rest
in a sloping vineyard and we leave it there, we
humans, to sink into elements in the earth, not
the proper place, but somewhere. You expect a savior
between the rows in a vineyard, really, feet
protected by sandals, but whose aren't in summer
in wine country? A boy in the Okanagan, I thought
I was the savior for a while, this was about
the time I was learning to read though I was reluctant
to talk. I was waiting for God to give me the news.
I was not ready but I wouldn't have said no, not
at first, anyway.

A Misspent Youth

Sometimes I thought it must be nice to be
dumb like those other kids, for example
the ones who could lie on the ground without
clutching rocks or grass because they didn't know
how fast the Earth was spinning through that nothing
nobody wanted to be lost in. Space, my mother said,
give me some space in my own kitchen, where light
begins each morning that arrives whether we pray
or don't. Why do you read books, the dumb kids
always asked me, not seeking an answer because
that's the way they were, so I never told them
it's because I'm looking for someone who's
smarter than I am, to get somewhere that you
are not. Out of this town, for example, which
some of them did despite everything, what
"moods and frowns and wrinkles strange"
I showed them, what utterly *useless* ways to
make myself less happy. Sometimes I thought
it must be easy to be dumb as dirt,
and you must get a lot more respect
from the soccer coach, a lot more bare tit
from girls like Katie.

I Have a History with Olives

When I was a kid I hated them. Not that they showed up much at our house, and maybe that's why. Somehow I learned to eat them. It was either before or exactly when I was stuck in Camp Borden for Christmas night 1954. I had done something wrong again, so I was confined to base while almost everyone else was off home or in town for Xmas. The mess hall had few eaters in it, and maybe I was feeling sorry for myself, or just trying to be George as usual, but for Christmas dinner I had a big platter just covered with olives.

That was my big adventure with olives. Once, riding along in a bus or something in southern Italy I saw that in an olive grove
they had put a big groundsheet under the olive tree and were apparently whacking the tree with sticks to make olives fall on the ground.

I think it was Kroetsch who wanted to come back as an olive tree, maybe with a hole in it.

The Maltese M

Surely it tells us something that more people
read *Paradise Lost* than even begin reading *Paradise
Regained*. Things used to be different, but now
more people say "Oh, Hell!" than say "Heavens
to Betsy!" Of course a lot of those nice old names
have fallen into disuse, like spats or sugar tongs.
I was thinking of reading some more Milton because
his name starts with M, as does Marlowe,
whom I am reading now after a long hiatus.
Have you ever noticed that hiati are getting
longer these days? And really, there isn't one,
not a true one, because I didn't read Marlowe
so much as be the kind of person who has
read Marlowe, who went sometimes as Merlin,
as does the wise wife of my longtime friend Dave
McFadden, whose books of poetry I have been reading
for all our adult lives. Dave believes that Paradise
is here right now, all around us, and so he
absorbs it and bears witness that life is not
all subway noise and undersalted eggs. Heavens
to Betsy, I say to him, more people confess
willingly to reading your books of poetry than
even know about *Paradise Regained* in any edition.
He smiles like a bodhisattva who will have
no specific religion until time leaks out under the door.

Bright

Does it bring any solace or calm to you
to know the sun is mortal, too? One day
far in the future or someone else's past
it will be a dark skeleton tumbling in black
space, its gleam long gone, and time some-
one else's job.
                It's happened before, and if
you think time is a big deal in rime, you
ought to imagine how long the poem has been
underway since Sol was a bright new babe.

He's The Guy

He's the guy they always want to be their keynote poet,
you know, who'll we get to headline this festival?
Has a flop of brown-grey hair like W.H. Auden
without the wrinkles. Know what I mean? Always
beats you out just when you feel the prize is yours.
People who read a little poetry love him, he tells them about
nature. And human nature, our shared views
of hayricks as opposed to the Wednesday pasta special.
Always shows up in floppy corduroys and big old hat,
Ready to dish up some Wallace Stevens without
the hangups.

        I imagine he lives a poet's life,
you know what I mean? Has a favourite tree he leans on,
will stare the sunrise in the eye till the rooster
wakes up. I hear he does something called a poets'
workshop. He can be spied hauling tools to work,
comes out for lunch with sawdust all over his eyelids.
Once he disappointed a visiting monarch. It wasn't
just the tie he would not wear, the Queen liked that.
It was that serious brooding country magazine face,
wouldn't break into a polite smile, made her brain
shuffle.

Fronds in Wind

Six hours after I gave the old old Mayan woman
a coin on Calle 58, I realized that she
is likely younger than I, that I
am needful of her years. I never saw her eyes,
all the brown legs went by relentlessly, that's the wrong
word but it will do with its secret energy, I have to get on to
what this wants me to say. There is an English professor
in Toronto who believes that poets know what to say and
they say it and they are in the centre of his
country and the subject of his lectures. Calle 58
is really important but it is not in literature,
its autobuses disgorge people, short ones, and no,
that is not a good enough verb. She is not the only
old woman sitting on a sidewalk. Like a fool
I said the word "mamacita," and touched
her hand – it was some kind of brown paper. If
I come by that same place tomorrow and she
is there, I will give her fifty-eight
times as much.

That night, while stepping out of the wonderful
noisy restaurant in my confusion I touched the costumed
waitress's hand. Her smile went down, then up.

—Mérida

Curiosity

The neonate looked up at me with eyes
I have known forever. Then clouds, white on top,
grey underneath, slid behind those eyes, the way
a dog methodically licks vanilla ice cream
out of a paper cup. I step all over images
people have left behind in their hurry
to get to the delicatessen, where a famous
admiral is sitting down to a heavy sandwich.
His eyes have seen dark clouds in a medicine chest,
dancing men on a moist deck; he eats with
decorum, his devotees at the window, hands
beside their eyes, hungry, and midsize in their
spring outfits. The baby knew I was there,
I know this for a certainty, its placid demeanor
no match for my anxiety, the quality
that has got me through a thousand confrontations.
If you have any desire to know my secret heart,
read on.
I hear it coming, we can divine
the cosmic weather's intentions by its ability
to imitate the peace beyond curiosity.

Canadian Life

Canadian life goes on. Trucks in the back alley
groan the way my cousin groaned when they finally
lifted the heavy machine off him. It's a national
question we are too busy to answer, holes appear
and we patch them with pavement, then more
holes appear, lines get longer at the credit union,
Canadian life goes on, sunlight caught in newspapers,
no question about it, Toronto really is interesting.

My cousin died anyway, not making the news, not
able to see his mother again, the traffic returned
to speed, I noticed a new hesitation in my father's walk.
My face is getting old faster than the sky is, Canadian
skies are among our favourite, as for example the sky
over southern Manitoba when you are twenty years old
and your moustache is coming in, the moustache that
surprised you by going white some years later, but

Canadian life goes on in the Big White, poetry seeps
into the prairies, my father chased my mother
through the kitchen, reading *Venus and Adonis* to her.
A lot of things are louder than Shakespeare, but now
we have mute buttons on everything, including boyfriends
with eyes for your car, soccer fans in the street,
Nova Scotia too far past the horizon to fret your
brow. I'll take a pill for Canadian life, and watch it
from the upstairs bedroom window, dear friends.

Father's Day

Trembling stalactites are an omen if you like—
a presentiment of something unknown is to be
expected. But are you likely to see any, likely
to hear their music? Dance with me, Henry. Not
as I heard this morning the 1953 music of Betty
Roché, and in this time of the easily awesome,
isn't that something?
                                    I've been in favour of
something all my life, even shepherd's thumb
is something. There will be plenty of time
for the absence of something, and did we not
hear the silent drop of a hammerhead on that note?
I'm older than the boy in 1953, who knew there was
a world no neighbourhood had even stopped to give
a song about. So when Billy Eckstine was faking it,
it was still it, a something you needn't even
ask your father about, your father you loved,
and who told you how to remember which were
stalactites, who spent his time in science and
let you handle fiction. He showed you how to
hold a hammer at the top end, a lesson about
fulcrum, one supposes. If he believed in omens
you never heard about it. If he only got to read about
things you would later go and see, well, they
ought to name a day for such a person.

Olde Valley Guy's Plaint

Was it scenery or furniture? I mean the
forest, alright, sparse trees on the hillside,
the lake covering something this generation
knew nothing about, the rocks spilled into
deltas now lichened. I guess the answer depends
on whether you are a citizen or a god
among others.

                Speaking of the lake and such,
how many times have I leaned over our rail,
biting a peach we brought down from
my home town?

[long pause]

Is this furniture, a notation by Death,
my acquaintance of long standing in dark grey,
or disbelief, scenery I greeted daily as earth's
unclarified demeanor?

                   Need everything now
be so obdurate for us citizens, obdurate
and never noticed by the gods we plead
our quiet cases to?

Big Glimmer

The ocean is always evaporating, he says, as if
he were Friedrich Nietzsche, human kind is no better,
I've reached a great age and no longer care what cars
look like, who's on the radio, only the light reflecting
from your skin, only the freshness of the bread, only
some third thing to make the rhetoric familiar. The ocean,
he says, offers so little, a thin surface you will break
at your risk, a history made up largely of defeat
or disappointment, as in soccer. Dogs get wet
and clamber into cars, real fish and chips
have pretty well disappeared save perhaps in
New Zealand. Yet the only awesome sight
I have seen was the immense curve of the Pacific
at midnight, lit by a moon a little higher than
this Boeing 747 newly entered the southern hemisphere.
My father was not in the window seat, though he
should have been, this wiry man who used to
wade into Lake Okanagan with a big white bar of soap.

Myth is History

The toilet paper I've used during my life—
do I owe the earth a tree? Two trees?
But wait, haven't my turds fed the earth,
or were they slid into the sea?

At the University of California someone said
we western civilization people have cut off nature,
returning our fertile product not to the earth
but into the ocean, where all the salt is, except
that in the peanut butter I bought today, a jar
otherwise free of additives. Think about salt
in your stomach, in your small intestine, think about
those Road movies, Crosby and Hope back to that sound stage
where extras keep putting on ruffled sleeves and moustaches,
their fecal discharge in the Bay, not leaking nutrients
into a sun-warmed pasture. Southern California poetry
too could use some advice from, was it Kantorowicz?
He said drop that basketball, pick up a hoe, and even your life.

The Red

I don't know how many stars I've seen implode,
and turn into dark orbs in your path if you're
tooling your way through black space out there,
so cold you might as well forget it, the way
you've forgotten what baby carrots taste like
till now when I've reminded you. So many things
in this universe are round if you look from
the appropriate angle, and so many things inside you,
round. Things get old enough, they're going to be
round, like rocks in a river bed. Though all day long
you can run hose water over a square rock,
you won't make it round in the slightest. But
start reading La Chartreuse de Parme, you'll age
after every page. I don't know how often I've
come home after a recognizance of the universe,
ours and the one next door, to find the carpet worn
a little between the front door and the fridge. Black
is the right shade for space. Any other colour and
who would want to go there?

A Late Smile

I was born in December, and now I'm in
the December of my life. Has anyone seen
what next year will be like or whether I'll
be there at all? I only know I don't want to
come to an end of hearing wonderful words like
sawhorse. I'm tempted here to go to seahorse
and ruin the singular surprise of that wood, to
seesaw, with Marjorie in the sea salt, that
girl with the curly somersault, my grandfather
in Somerset could have taught her. This silliness
a poet in San Francisco may have taught me
was all right, sawdust work around barns being so
far from ephemeral, which sounds, doesn't it,
like a medicine you have to earn your way to
by growing old.

No Demands

"Death has not required us to keep a day free."
—Samuel Beckett, *Proust*

Whenever it is convenient, he says,
wry smile in the dark we can't see where his face
ought to be
                  under that hood we learned as children
to hate and envy.

That hood is the amount of astronomy
they will know after
                  we've gone.

Don't bother your pretty little head about it
he says, and we can hear his breath like an aqualung
in an echo chamber,
                  or so
we fancy.

So we fill our days
                  or allow them to fill
with inconsequence, not exactly planning
to continue till
                  to our surprise
the fellow is here. No, he will
make no demands whatsoever.

I'll Be There

It's not so much how can I leave it
but rather how can it go on without me.
The world, I mean. I used to think it was
all around me, but now I know it goes
through me, I'm like you, lover, a mesh in water.
Or rather water in water, water that can think.
Even thought will fill the logos when I'm somewhere
else, but come to think of it, how can I be?
People will say he's gone, how sad, how diminished
this all is, but I'll be there, just you'd say
disassembled. It hurt so badly when I was born
that I commenced at once to forget it. I made
my mother forget the pain and cup my big hairless head
in her teenaged hand. Now she tells me all about
her pains once a week, it even hurts to hold
the telephone. She hints about heading elsewhere
but not tonight, she says. It's not so much
how can she leave us but rather how damned old
I'll be when I'm an orphan. My hair, my whiskers,
my thumbnails are growing as fast as bamboo,
I'm turning into a Japanese garden, that's where
I will be when they all think I've left the planet.

Inside the Tent

In grades one and two I lived with my parents and sister in Greenwood, B.C., a cute little town that was billed as "Canada's smallest city," because it had been a going concern around the turn of the century, before the world price of copper bottomed out. I didn't know it at the time, but we were about eight miles from the U.S. border.

There were a lot of things I didn't know when I was five or six years old. But I knew that there was a war going on in Europe and Asia, and we used chalk and the sidewalk to draw fighter planes as seen from the side. I knew that my father had tried to get into the army but they wouldn't let him in, so he taught cadets to fire rifles. That was the war for this family.

The war was a bit odd for us kids living in Greenwood. When I was in grade two a thousand Japanese people from somewhere moved into town, filling up the houses and stores that had gone empty for a few decades. We European kids shared a lot of misinformation about the new Japanese kids: for example, I somehow got the impression that when Japanese families had twin boys, one of the brothers had to be sacrificed on an outdoor stone altar. I guess I was mixing the Bible story of Isaac into my own locale. A few years later, in Oliver, I had a new classmate named Isaac, and I was still filled with a mixture of horror and pity for him.

But I also had a Japanese dentist in Greenwood, and his name was George. Years and years later, in Bill Hoffer's bookstore, I met a man who knew the dentist George something. Let's say Nakamura. I remember that he had to pull one of my teeth, and the freezing didn't take. I stayed away from dentists till I was so old that I had to get implants that broke the bank.

Among the things I knew was that my father had moved us from Peachland to Greenwood for a teaching job at the big old school there. I also knew that teachers had to get other jobs during the summer, so my father got a job as a fire lookout on top of a mountain somewhere. I thought that it was between Greenwood and Grand Forks, because the forest fire headquarters were in Grand Forks.

Here is where my memory has a little tangle in it. Down at the end of our short street there was a tee intersection, and right there was a big house where my "girlfriend" lived. But then, when my father got a job looking for smoke, my "girlfriend" was the warden's daughter, and they must have lived in Grand Forks. Not that it mattered all that much, because I understood then and understand now that "girlfriend" had a reason to be inside quotation marks.

Early in the summer my father took my dog Caesar to be with him for a week or two on top of his mountain. Then a little later, in August, I think, he took me. We slept in a tent, on beds made of pine boughs. Outside, we had a black iron stove for cooking. I have a photo of me stirring the pot on that stove, with a band of pheasant feathers around my head. I remember burning my knee a little on that stove.

I also banged my head on the steel butt of my father's rifle. I guess I have always been accident-prone. I know that I would not climb higher than about five rungs on the jackpine ladder that my father used to reach the wobbly lookout shack high up in the air. I was really afraid that he would come crashing down on the mountain top rocks, and then what would I do for him? I was six and a half.

Then came the day on which my father had to go down the mountain alone to get groceries and mail. He told me that I was in charge of the mountain, and he told me it would be a good idea to stay in the tent. Not far away there was a natural bowl in the rock, where we washed and my father shaved. During the long hours when my father was off the mountain, I thought about that stone bowl full of cold water. I had once seen a ground squirrel washing his face there. At night, after my father had turned off the kerosene lamp, I imagined larger animals coming to drink or wash.

I stayed in the tent for hours, feeling the sun's heat despite our altitude, and later closing the tent flap when darkness came. Sometimes when I remember this time I remember my father arriving hours after sunup the next day. But really—would a father let his kid stay on a mountain all night? Well, back in those days we expected kids to learn things faster, and while we did make sure they got their vaccinations, we didn't make them wear helmets while riding their bicycles.

Here's what I did during those hours in the tent. I read comic books. I read my regular book, too, but I read about half a dozen comic books, read them slowly and read them over again. I got them on loan from that ranger's daughter who was supposed to be my "girlfriend", though I don't recall seeing her very often if at all. I had never seen comic books before. I guess they had them in Grand Forks, or maybe she got them when her family went across the line to Spokane. They were something like the weekend coloured comics in the Vancouver *Province*. Some people called them the funnies, but I thought that was a bit English or something.

I liked them a lot, and I would become an inveterate comic book reader in years to come. I loved the panels, the curved corners of them. I don't remember what any of these comics were, but I know that I would always prefer real people to half-dressed animals, Terry Lee to Donald Duck.

I probably dozed off in the tent, with a comic book in my hand. But I think I was awake when I heard a noise outside. I knew within a few seconds that this was not my father come back. I heard little bits of twigs and tarpaulin, a clink. I heard snuffling at the corner of my tent, a little bit of heavy snuffling, and then in a few seconds, nothing more.

I stayed quiet and tried to go back to my reading. But I knew something I had not known before. I knew that when I got older I was going to be something different, something I didn't know about yet. Didn't know about poetry yet.

La Manzanilla Quatrains

for Ted and Linda

1.

We strolled around Marina Vallarta,
sneering at huge white boats from Delaware.

Before the Argentine meat restaurant stood
a Buenos Aires *chica*, what cloth and dare!

2.

Is that a jonquil, I asked, a jacaranda?
There's the semitropic I read,

the local I walk around in, some place
in coastal Jalisco, *flores* I need.

3.

These Jalisco ants adore my flesh
as I adore the red snapper's skin

crisp, painted with *chile*, lying
steps from the sea with others in.

4.

Signs ask us not to swim, see these
cocodrillos? They move only to feed.

They will never be Mexican villagers,

have no *corazón*, no musical need.

5.

Each night we dine not on the side-
walk but in the very street.

The fish give up their crispy
skin, their lately swimming meat.

6.

Papayas ripen one by one
just out of reach in the back

garden behind breakfast

where we all go crack, crack.

7.

Fish tacos are thirteen pesos,
or as we Gringos say, free.

The home-made *chipotle* sauce
has made Jalisco out of me.

8.

Jarritos, qué bueno son, here
nearly half a century in, small

jolts brought me by sleeping dogs,

bright red *bebidas*, all, all, all.

9.

Above the wet blue sky circle
birds not squeaking on our *palapa* wall—

pelicans, vultures, frigates, *gaviotas*,
not our friends at all, not at all.

10.

The most innocent eyes in town
where pickup trucks with loudspeakers cruise

are on these blowfish newly dead
on shining sand, our latest news.

11.

Church bell clanks twenty-eight times,
once for each dog lying in the road.

Blood drips on my white tennis sock,
and scatters to every insect's abode.

12.

What is that fuchsia plant, and what
is that fuchsia, is it flower or leaf?

Do I live too in its assumed place
in a confidence of knowledge or belief?

13.

The squashed frog and the flattened snake
acquire more tire tracks by the day.

The fish seem more delicious while
the Gringos grow brownish and grey.

14.

Really? Coconuts in the back yard?
Coconuts and papayas on trees?

We are very far away, very far
from the Quebecker playing spoons on knees

15.

No U.S. hotels. no U.S. hamburgers,
no ski-jets at the beach, *U.S.A. Today*

isn't here yet. I think that smiling *niño*
is poor, yes, but not poor in San Jose.

Jan. 19 – Feb. 2, 2012.

The Swimming Hole

Growing up as a kid in the South Okanagan, you expected to be in swimming most days between early May and late September, unless school and/or work made that hard to do. I lived in Oliver, B.C., in a kind of desert, but surrounded by swimming sites.

Probably the most popular of these was Tuc-el-Nuit Lake, which was not then surrounded by houses. It is the only lake I have ever swum across, so you can see how small it is. Back in those days it would freeze over in the winter, and we used to skate on it, enjoying the pings we heard in the ice in front of us. But in the summer, even though kids said it was bottomless, it was for swimming, and the few top inches of the water would be as warm as the coffee I am just now finishing. There was a lot of that green muck in it too, because it was connected to the river somehow.

Just north of Tuc-el-Nuit were two small lakes called Gallagher Lake and Mud Lake. Mud Lake was shallow and full of reeds, and all we did there was fish for yellow perch, but the south end of Gallagher Lake was our second most popular swimming place. There was a high rock cliff all along the east side. Highway 97 was just barely invisible up to the west. Apparently the nuns who ran the hospital in town lived at the north end. We never went there. But the south end of Gallagher Lake was a great place to gather, and in those days there were no drugs and sex at the beach. I even went there with my pal Fred Van Hoorn after he somehow acquired my girlfriend Barbara.

If anyone had a car, or if we were hanging out with our parents, we would go to the beach at the bottom of the main street in Osoyoos. Osoyoos Lake was bigger than any Oliver lakes. The U.S. border ran right across it, and I don't think we ever went swimming south of the border. We were always interested in impressing Osoyoos girls, but the rumour was that they were mostly "Yankee bait." The nice thing about the beach in Osoyoos was that you had a choice of grass or sand when you were out of the water, having a cigarette or Mission Orange or something.

I never knew anyone who went swimming in Vaseaux Lake,

a few miles north of Gallagher. I once went canoeing on Vaseaux Lake, and promised myself that I would do it again, but that was a promise I never kept. The next Lake up was Dog Lake, at Okanagan Falls, but I don't remember swimming there. Late on Graduation Night I came to to discover that I was sitting on the back of a horse for the first time in my life, and almost falling off frontward because the horse was drinking out of Dog Lake.

At the other end of Dog Lake was the less used of Penticton's two long and sandy beaches. We went there a few times, but we were much more likely to use the beach that was next to downtown, the north beach, at the bottom of Lake Okanagan. This was my favourite beach. When you sat in the sand and looked north you could see that the lake was bordered by clay cliffs on either side. You could see but not grasp the melted glacier's immense age. Looking more closely, you could see that the grains of sand were of many colours, some red, some black, some white, and so on. About three hundred feet off shore were big moored rafts, to which you swam and from which you dived. At the east end of the beach was a giant peach, inside which teenaged girls were stationed to sell you ice cream cones.

The temperature was somewhere in the nineties. There were hotrods parked at the curb. Almost all the girls were blonde. Is it any wonder that we grew up feeling more like California than Ontario?

They built a swimming pool in Oliver when I was a kid. It was always opened officially for the May 24th weekend, but for some reason there would be water in it well before that. So we would climb over the fence and get an unsupervised swim, the kind any kid likes best. I think a lot of us peed while we were in the pool. What are the odds? We managed to feel up the girls or at least press our bodies against them. There was green sludge in the water, as there was in any swimming water around town. Once a week the pool would be drained, and a kid was hired to clean it out, with big brushes on handles. Ronnie Carter had the job until he quit for some reason, and my parents suggested that I would be ideal for the job. I got to keep the things I found in the green sludge, coins and bracelets and so on. It took hours to clean that pool in the 95-degree sun. I got sunstroke and wound up in the hospital for a while. Now, sixty years later I like the sunshine but I can't be out in it with no hat.

I think they built the pool partly to keep us kids away from the swimming hole in the river just down the hill from the Oliver Theatre. My parents told me I was never to go swimming in the river, and I think that a lot of parents felt that way. But there was no grass near the river at the swimming hole, so there must have been a lot of foot traffic around there. Sometimes in the movies shown at the Oliver Theatre there would be a bucolic scene of American boys cavorting at the ol' swimming hole, with a rope for swinging out over the water and letting go.

But the Okanagan River is fast and as they say treacherous. There was a kid who was supposed to be the best swimmer in town, and he drowned there, or rather downstream. Seems he was sitting on a chair in the water for some reason, and he just disappeared. Though I used to go down to the swimming hole sometimes, I don't remember trying to swim there.

But once in some evening sunshine I was down at the swimming hole. I don't remember whether any other kids were there. I was probably watching myself having an imagined adventure involving spies or secret interstellar visitors. Then I saw a man and woman, he in a suit and she in a dress with a belt around her waist, with their arms around one another, walking toward the quick-moving green river, walking then into the river, never pausing, walking until they were deep into the river and gone, downstream.

I looked around, but saw that I was the only witness to this scene. Since that time I have had numerous ideas about what might have been going on. But that night while I was waiting for sleep I had the edges of a familiar feeling—that I was going to have to be something like a poet when I grew up.

Ace on the Ground

At five-thirty in the morning I stopped reading Reznikoff and Stan started reading Plato; it was that kind of commune.

Ten years earlier we met for the first time, in San Francisco; he came to the door young and naked and it wasn't his door.

He didn't exactly look like all those statues he'd seen in Italy when he was a Navy teen, hairy and dark-eyed.

And I was luckier in later years, lucky too to read his eager poems, straight talk, bent news, sensible oddity.

When he renounced poetry two worlds had to adjust, news could cease to be news, tyrants flinch.

For seventy years he's been talking in a Chicago accent he must have made up, a kid named Stan, hard to imagine, asphodel journalist.

He once said Hockey Night in Canada became beautiful when the arena fogged up and stopped the money.

Then he took Berlin the way others took speed, a city where Jews can walk the *strasse* without wearing a star or history's pants.

Where you can wear a pink thing if you so desire, and what does desire need in any case—a book launch?

How many times had Warren pulled out another case of Carling Black Label Beer, that pivot, that generous citizenship.

Meaning a poet divinely inspired can write tragedy alone or comedy alone, poor captive, poor splendid drainpipe.

But with *technê* can the poet write tragedy and can he write comedy, and rising with first light leave both new in the old world.

With a familiar smile, with a gleaming head that is both dome and bone, naked sense arrives at the real door.

Magic Mitt

When he went back for a foul popup behind third base, all of us York Street Tigers and all the Domtar guys shut their eyes tight.

He had such a sweet disposition that dogs wanted to *be* him, other drivers forgave him, and the Russian language spoke itself.

It's not that he made you glad to be alive—it's just that he let you know you were alive.

I made fun of him for reading all the novels written by British women, and now I think I'd better get at it, starting with Rose Tremaine.

I met him in the Fifties, when all the famous people had his initials — Mickey Mantle, Marilyn Monroe, Mary Martin, Mickey Mouse.

We mailed each other letters every week, complaining about the latest communication devices.

At university he was famous for his barbaric yawp, and so was Walt Whitman, who had his initials upside down.

Kids loved him because he liked dimes so much, he'd give a kid a quarter for a shiny dime.

I think Carol Matthews handled the household expenses. Mike Matthews made the coffee and you'd better not put sugar in it.

I saw him on the stage, I saw him on television, I saw him on the page, but he was at his very best in the parking lot—don't ask.

I knew we'd love each other forever when our daughters beat us in a game of two-on-two basketball.

In Montreal I admired him for walking around lower Westmount's biggest block before having the third dessert.

He often started a sentence with the word "Look," and by golly, it felt like exactly the right thing to do.

He was my fraternity brother, the only one I ever knew, the man with the golden sword and the magic mitt, my secret gentle sibling.

Poetry and Painting

Seventeen is a beautiful prime number, and 17 *rue Campagne-Première* was where *Atelier 17* was, and so was Pierre.

When he enters my house on 11th Avenue I forget that he was a student at the *Académie Julian*, I hope he passed.

In Montreal I sit on my friend Howard's back sundeck and look over the fence of Lower Canada College, where Pierre went to school.

Seventy is a good number too, the lowest weird number; my friends slip over seventy and their voices are twenty-seven.

Eleven is a prime number, and Pierre is welcome inside my door any day of the week.

He does not work as a sculptor, but according to his name he should be a powerful artist's carved stone.

I knew a mad woman who heard Pierre's voice in her head, Leonard's voice and Pierre's voice, two great voices.

When Pierre and Pete and Dan and Milty started the scurrilous underground newspaper they were a long way from L.C. College.

What a fine French nose he has grown after all these years; with that nose he should be president of the republic.

So elegant a man, how could he be a Georgia Straight hippie, how could he be a North Vandal poet?

Painting abstract, you are out there on your own, where no one can think of what to say about what you leave for us.

I watched as he came back with a yellow feather; I watched him come back with blood.

I watched his bony painter's hand, it was one of six hands on Robin's casket, above the grass.

Poetry and painting continue to be companions, the river propels sound toward the sea, everything is deep enough.

Tiles Spiral

No one has ever been so gracious and meaty in black leather and feathers, boots and perspiration.

No preposition has ever been so toward as her into, her from, her below, her much before.

She long ago befriended a lopsided muse who gave her an eye the dumb-ass writers did not desire

She can read French if it is difficult enough to satisfy her ocelot curiosity.

Gilles Deleuze stepped out of her path, lifted his hat to show scant hair, and whispered bienvenue.

You are, he murmured through that other language, something incomprehensible in our world.

She taught us the razorblade trick, and now the courageous few are Scott free.

Superman adores her. Great Scott, Clark Kent always cries, where the eff are you?

She has stepped in high heel boots into the street with energy that must follow *une nuit blanche*.

She's in a telephone booth in Kingston, superhero duds on the floor around her feet.

You'll find her under glass on the Boulevard de Bercy, or you will not find her, here she is.

Because the map too is unstable, we can depend on that, we will see Scott issue the very paper we need.

Auntie Pam

Auntie Pam always, till the end of her life, spoke with an English accent. So when I was a boy I had to put aside my normal antipathy to the English for her, just as I did with my grandfather, who liked to use English expressions, though he had left the "Old Country" as a boy and returned only once for a visit. Aunty Pam, I eventually learned, was brought up in semi-rural New Westminster. Maybe her parents spoke with an English accent.

She was the tall young bride of my Uncle Gerry, the youngest kid in his family. When I first knew her she was often to be seen in her army outfit. In fact during some visit I must have made to her family home, I was photographed wearing her army hat and jacket and sporting her army purse or bag or whatever they called it. In the same roll of film there is a picture of her giving me a piggyback ride. I think she was getting to know the Bowering family.

Okay, I was ten years old and getting interested in women's chests. We had moved into the village of Oliver, and it was a lot different from living in orchard houses as we had done for the past two years. Now we had neighbours instead of apple trees next to us. On the west side were the Wilkinses—Chick Wilkins, Mrs Wilkins and Darryl Wilkins, their son who was a couple years older than I, a kid who always wanted to be the robber when we played cops and robbers. I had a little bedroom on the west side of our little house, and a window that looked across at Mr and Mrs Wilkins's bedroom.

I didn't spend much time at that window, even in the winters, when house lights were used from the late afternoon. I was inherently shy, and believed that God was watching anyway. I spent more time with my copies of *Sport* magazine and paperback westerns from the cornerstore.

But I did get at least one good look, which was not easy, because there was a Siberian elm tree between our houses, and Mrs Wilkins's window was not exactly opposite mine. It was nice and dark in my room; my parents probably thought that I was reading under the covers with my flashlight. Oh please, oh please, I said inside my head, and then felt guilty because you usually said that to God inside your head, and this was not God's business I was on.

And then there they were! Not bare, not that much good luck. But there they were, in a bright white brassiere, I looked and looked, telling myself to quit looking, until Mrs Wilkins disappeared from that part of her room, and I gave up. But I saw them and they were next door, large, lifted in all their weight to points. I had seen Jane Russell in the straw of some barn I would never see, seen her, that is, in ads for the movie *The Outlaw* a few years ago, when I was around seven. It was confusing for a boy who was starting a career of reading westerns. Was she somehow the outlaw? I thought that I might get it when I was older. The movie never came to Oliver, and I figured that if it did I was not going to be allowed to watch it. Mrs Wilkins was more real than any movie, anyway, even with the elm tree in the way.

But Aunty Pam was family. I didn't have to peek through a window at Auntie Pam. She was just as pretty as Mrs Wilkins or Jane Russell, and I got to see her often because she and Uncle Gerry lived in the Valley, and our families visited each other more than those of any other relatives I had.

I was shy all the time around Auntie Pam, because she was making me feel my skin in a way I didn't know all that well. Part of the time I was stealing a look at her, and the rest of the time I was making sure I didn't look at her so that she wouldn't think I was looking at her. Now that she is dead and I am an old guy, I wonder whether she had a pretty good clue what that pre-pubescent nephew was going through. Whether she enjoyed it a little.

Anyway, soon after my aunt and uncle were married they were living in Kelowna, that strange little town you had to take a ferry to, up there in the north Okanagan. My sister was born in Kelowna, which made it a little more familiar, and when I was ten I got to stay with Uncle Gerry and Auntie Pam for a week. Of course, this was before they had their four kids, so I must have been a little mysterious, or maybe someone to practise on.

Uncle Gerry was ten years younger than my father, and kind of spirited, according to the stories my grandmother told me. She said that my father used to perform peculiar stunts from time to time, but "Gerald," perhaps because he was the youngest, was always up to something. I was kind of shy around their little house in Kelowna, of course, but liked watching the newlyweds, never wondering whether my parents had been like them.

As I said, I liked glimpsing Auntie Pam. She wore shirts with collars and buttons, nothing like the sexy garb of later generations. But I kept my eye peeled. I knew what I would be able to see if my eyesight and imagination got together. My model for a perfect female chest came from Al Capp's "Li'l Abner" cartoon, especially the characters Daisy Mae and Moonbeam McSwine. A year or so later, when I started drawing cartoons, I drew chests like theirs.

One day in the kitchen, Uncle Gerry snuck up behind Auntie Pam and put his arms around her and grabbed her breasts with his big hands. He made a comic growl. I turned my eyes away, but I couldn't do the same for my memory.

Auntie Pam had never taken care of a young boy before. She was probably pretty good with breakfast and lunch, but I don't remember. What I do remember is the bath.

I was sitting in the bathtub, the water not as high as it was in movies and comic strips, because this was the real world and the Okanagan Valley.

I washed my face, my arms, my chest, my legs, and so on, and I was probably thinking about Terry and Hotshot Charlie and the Dragon Lady, when a knock came to the bathroom door, and whether she had the door open a crack, I don't remember, but Auntie Pam asked me in her English voice, "Do you want me to scrub your back?"

Because she was new at this, I guessed. No, I didn't want her in there washing my bare back. No no no, I had never faced such a problem. "Yes, please," I said.

And she did. I don't know what she saw. I have no idea to this day what she may have been thinking. I have always assumed that she was innocently and vigorously interested in good English healthiness. It didn't take long, that back-scrubbing.

But I knew that I would never forget. That wonderful chest that really belonged to Uncle Gerry, right there in the bathroom with me. At that moment, or later that evening, I knew that I was going to be some kind of something when I got older.

Los Pájaros de Tenacatita

The *fulcro* (fulcrum) is a verse form I learned from the example of the Cuban-American poet Pablo Medina. It can be seen in his bilingual volume *Points of Balance / Puntos de Apoyo*. (Four Way Press, 2005). The middle couplet bears a discernible relationship to the first couplet and to the third couplet, but the third couplet need not be seen or heard in relationship with the first couplet. Pablo Medina said that with the fulcrum he wanted to get both the dialectic of the sonnet and the image of the haiku.

Breathing In

White pigeons on the corrugated
church roof, *alas*, they fold

wings beyond his language.
Words arrive on a Brazilian

jet liner, dropping like
spent insects onto his page.

Age Old

Laila may be four years old,
the puppy in her hands in front

of her chest, six weeks old.
His old *manos* remember two

Chihuahuas, ignorant of the
life they were always saving.

Blue Handkerchief

Watching blue sky *como* Pablo
Medina, he finds an aesthetic

made of frigate birds saying
nothing. Great is their height,

humble is *Jesús* in his passion
along the church's inside walls.

Cows, Fish

Beef Wellington on a rooftop,
punto de apoyo. gringo economy

clear as tomorrow morning's
nets in the sea. Mexicans there

are more beautiful, they are young,
they have children.

He Sets His Watch

6:20 every night the black and
yellow critters gather in two trees

then pulse in groups of ten
straight at his face and over

his soul if he still has one,
knowing he has never been a bird.

The Cowboy

It is difficult to seat a woman
in voluminous wedding dress

atop even a patient braided horse
in front of our little *iglesia*.

Where he has never knelt nor
has he crossed himself or swords.

A Silly Rime

Five Norwegian babes at the beach
have trios of clear assets each

from which he turns his gaze away
to follow the pelicans in the bay,

how they fold their *alas* and then they dive
for ocean's bounty to keep them alive.

Years at Sea

The graveyard between ocean and
crocodile enclosure offers a place

to sit and rest his lungs, air
sustaining meat with wings above

a stretch of sand unsullied yet
by Japanese earthquake detritus.

No Puede Ver

This oblique man, insect itches
up and down both legs, he

is partly here on the beach:
how little he really knows

of Japan, of earthquakes, of unseen
mosquitos, the flat of his hand.

No Ideas

Es reposado on this yellow deck,
sufficiently protected from sobriety,

ears attentive to abstract words,
he can't read the price on the bottle

to gauge how good all this is,
all this untoward restfulness.

Evening Sculpture

Laila's sister teaches her arithmetic,
pulling her hair when she looks

across the street. Where the gringas
work the blender, drink the numbers

memorized from the book in the kitchen
where *las mujeres* come and go.

Orion's Boy

Pelicanos dive into *pescadores'* nets
because that's where the fish are.

Then the four men gather to free
and let fly, an astral version

of catch and release. Our sky here
records all of this in specks of fire.

Marine Life

She sells sea shells by the
sea shore and she's in on

the joke. Come back *mañana*
he says, and she has more of them

than he could hope for, this
venera from the far ocean north.

5 – 0

His white plastic chair ten
meters from the touch line

at the *campo de deportes* became
a goal for the three-year-old

futbolistas behind him. How bright
they were, how drab the big pitch.

Solucionista del Rey

Wings beyond his language, *des-*
graciadamente, fold, and the fire

told springs from the sea, glints
for a moment and is gone, like

a simile into an immense la-
cuna no one will ever translate.

Or the Pot

How little he loves the world,
not the thing, but the idea.

A sweet hummingbird, for example,
smallest Buddhist on Earth, never

stays long enough for a complete
sentence, never counts the syllables.

Oriente

That frigate bird nipped that silver
fish and lifted that duck off his

feet from the hard wet sand, where
Japan may reach this coming

June, recall last year's *tsunami*,
a wharf at a time, a light bulb, too.

Psyche

His soul, if he still has one,
is softer on the edges, in

Melaque the gringos lock their
bicycles, hummingbirds stay away.

He remembers the Aztecs, how
butterflies indicate sexual flowering.

Stout Cortez

Caterwauling radio next door, no
bird in sight but the boy in the yard

sweeping, as willing to say hello
as any teenager anywhere, hello

America, is it all settled? Did
those bastards get all the gold?

So Much Depends

That unfortunate duck that rimed
so nicely not at all turned out

to be a booby with white feet
that lately stand for comfort

beside a wounded pelican, now
they say, fed fish by this companion.

Renaissance Verse

At the cappuccino shop he
and a lone sparrow share bun

and icing, bird as quick in this heat
as any Philip in the snow.

He, though, will plod uphill toward
a well-fed, well-caffeinéd nap.

Last Day Home

*Por supuesto las campanas de la
iglesia son puertos de su sueño*

into this agave afternoon, plastic
chairs in sand, seabirds unaware

of his homeland, he honours these *Indios*,
how they have borne this European weight.

La Manzanilla del Mar, Jalisco, January 2013

Somebody's Horse

The Southern Okanagan Valley of British Columbia is very dry—a desert, in fact, where water has to be cared for, where they had to build a canal called "the Ditch" to irrigate orchards, and where you were instructed to flush your toilet, if you had a flush toilet, only when it seemed absolutely necessary. You never brushed your teeth, and your father never shaved, with a running faucet.

But the valley used to be the path of a glacier that moved slowly in the southward direction taken by the Okanagan River now. You can see the presence of this extremely old news in the tall clay banks on both sides of Okanagan Lake at its south end, or in the striations in the rock faces as you go further south, toward Oliver, where I lived from Grade 3 to Grade 12. A kid living in the Southern Okanagan lived among signs of an ancient land, even while keeping track of the ground in front of him because he might be stepping where rattlesnakes now wanted to be.

The Valley is shaped the way a valley should be, so that you can stand at the intersection of Oliver's Main Street and Fairview Road, for example, and look up to the west and up to the east and see parallel lines of hills and then mountains. The river runs through the middle of the valley. Then on either side you now get orchards or vineyards; or in some cases you still get slopes of dusty soil with dry grass and sagebrush, right up until the hills rise seriously. The further you go up those hills and then into the mountains, the more likely you are to find pine trees, and in the winter you will, if you keep climbing, find your share of romantic snow.

As often as I could, when I was not working, when I was still a Wordsworthian boy, I would be up in those hills, east or west, watching for rattlesnakes or cactus, sometimes carrying an orange and a book that would fit into a pocket, walking around and looking for animal footprints. During the winter, when the water was turned off, I would explore the Ditch, sometimes on foot, sometimes with my bike. With your bike you could ride up and down the sloping concrete sides, but there was a problem when the ditch had to cross a road—it would change from concrete to some sort of metal, and there would be planks across the top, so you had to take your bike out and down across the road and up again and so on.

There was also a problem with the slime. There was a lot of green slime in the water of the southern Okanagan—in the lakes and in the river, in the town swimming pool and in the Ditch. Usually I walked when I was exploring the newly emptied Ditch. Once I found a necklace made of Dutch coins. Once I found a small-calibre pistol. Despite the fact that we were only fifteen miles from the U.S. border, this was the first pistol I had ever seen. The handgrip was missing, but the rest was there. Maybe it was a .22, I don't know. Once I found a big old primitive-looking jackknife with a toad sticker. I still have it, but I don't know what happened to the pistol or the necklace.

Up in the hills I found stuff, too. Some of it was stuff I had secretly buried a year or two earlier, my secret caches that included hunting knives I had found, baseballs, I can't remember what else. I found a lot of footprints, as I said, horseshoe prints, paw prints. In my fancy under the hot sun I liked to intermingle this business with the stuff I was reading in drugstore paperbacks by Max Brand. Sometimes I would find a tuft of fur on a barbwire fence, fur or hair. There was no one else around, unless I had brought my little old dog Dinky with me, but I tried to look knowledgeable and laconic, eyes squinted and lifted to scan the near horizon.

I found an old stove door once, and a woman's boot that must have come from the late nineteenth century. I found lots of rusty old cans that must have been emptied near a campfire decades before. I found mysterious square bottles from the olden days. I found skulls, big ones and small ones, from cows and birds and coyotes, maybe.

Once when I didn't have Dinky with me, I climbed a hillside cliff made of rotting stone just for fun, and on the other side there was a little open space of no trees and no rock outcroppings, kind of like a natural corral, natural except for the remains of a wooden fence. In the middle was a dead horse.

The body had been around so long that it didn't give off that smell you hate. In fact it was pretty well flat, some brown hide with the insides all gone, eyes gone, not like a sheepskin or bearskin, because it was just horsehide lying full length on the ground where the brown grass had all been removed.

There were horse buns all around, been there a long time in the sun, if you picked one up it would fall apart between your fingers. I stood and stared at my first dead horse. The flat neck still had a rope tied around it, and the rope was secured to a fence post. It looked so flimsy that I wondered why the horse had not pulled it loose.

Quite often in those days you might see large birds with long black wings circling around something in the hills, as in western movies or comic strips. I thought that they had probably been over this spot quite a long time ago. Since then the sun had made it a tannery.

I tried not to think about the person who had tied the rope and why he had not come back. Was he saving a bullet? Did something happen to him? Had he ever given this horse a name?

After I descended into the valley and went home to fill the sawdust hopper and so on, I didn't tell anyone about the place where I'd seen something wrong. I knew that I was going to be something, a poet or something.

The Crows

Translated and then some from the French of Arthur Rimbaud

1. The poet addresses God, introduces meat metaphor
Ah Lord, when the prairie is frozen hard,
when deep inside this hambone slaughterhouse,
we hear the slow angelus you peel for us . . .
over the poor deflowered garden
like a butcher your giant mouth sends
these sad dear delicious crows.

2. The poet sends the crows far into the past
Oh strange army with your severe cries,
like icy wind attacking our nipples!
You in your long slow ebony flight
along the routes of ancient calvaries,
past all the fossils, past those yet undiscovered,
disperse yourselves, my friends, rally once again!

3. The crows circle space and time, free of the poet
Past millponds, over the fields of France,
or sleeping the deaths of long-lost years,
it's time to turn about, is it not true, winter will
throw aside every whispered repentence!
Yours are the donkey's cries of duty,
oh, you our funereal black feathers!

4. The poet calls on the birds to get it over with
But, dear saints of the sky, above our smog,
mates long disappeared into the enchanted night,
leave behind the frivolity of Spring,
descend deep into the enchained forest,
under the grass beyond the frowning world,
dive into the undoing beyond all exit.

North

You should hear an old Inuit man
            say "Bullshit!"
                        in an Inuvik bar.

Name in a Fort Smith graveyard:
            Suzanne Klawhammer
                        —1931.

            [Later I saw her picture in the museum.
            She is with two dogs. Her name is spelled
            Susan Clawhammer. Brother Saurraut
            says she went with them every morning
            for water, and that she was a good woman.]

Hay River is the real and unacknowledged capital of the North West.

That's what they say in Hay River.

            [People all over the north are resentful
            of the misrepresentation of the north in
            southern media. Especially the notion
            that people go up there who can't cope
            in the south.]

The northernmost areas of the Mackenzie

are called "down north."

When you leave the north
          you go "out."

Hard Under, High Above

Once in a while you bite your tongue
or a rock goes down the hillside wrong,

the earth itself tips not quite right
and nobody notices, but you notice;

your sister ought to notice but she's
watching ancient game shows on TV.

Your sister and you have the same scabs
on the same portions of your lower limbs

but she will never stand on a stage and
exhibit them for a slim public regard

though she is slim herself, what you'd call
witchy gaunt, came years ago sliding

out the birth canal you'd made your
rough way. Once in a while you bite your

knuckle in a blend of fear and regret,
or sudden newts want to cross the road

unattended by sound of any kind,
those purblind sojourners, poor rubber

tongues crawling over the macadam
between somewhere and somewhere else

for no reason perceivable by this driver
intent on the curvature of the earth

or his spine while he stands on two feet
puzzled by his ability, biting the bullet.

The Giant Snowball

The other day while Jean was driving us to lunch with my childhood pal Willy, I saw three boys on a front lawn fingertipping a volleyball to each other in the afternoon sunshine. It made me momentarily happy, and I remarked to Jean that it was a welcome change—more commonly these days one would see three young heads bent over small screens. I didn't care that this happened while the Olympic games were being contested. Those boys, as far as I could tell while our car drove past them, were not contesting—they were just playing, and relying on one another for fun.

We sure did that when I was an elementary school boy. In Oliver our school had a girls' playground to its south and a boys' playground to its north. Either playground was made up of about ten acres of semi-arid land, mostly composed of sand and rocks, with sagebrush and antelope brush and greasewood growing slowly and sparsely. There were rattlesnakes and cactus to watch out for, but that was true in just about every vacant lot in Oliver. Occasionally we had rattlesnakes in our back yard, down the hill from the school.

In those days the boys in Oliver usually played "swords." We had wooden swords that would be held to us by our belts, hardly ever any shields, once in a while cardboard box armour. Sometimes we made bows and arrows, but we seldom used them against each other, because really, you could put an eye out, just as our parents said. We snaffled laths from the lumberyard and employed them as javelins, but only if the other guys had cardboard shields.

Swordfights went on all over town, and sure enough, boys did come home with skinned knuckles and a bit of blood in the crew cut. But the parents usually knew as well as we did that we boys made up the rules around here and agreed to them.

We saw in the comic books that kids back east made snow forts in the winter. We usually didn't get enough snow for any such thing, but we made another kind of fort in that big boys' playground north of the school. It took a lot of teamwork and time to make them. To begin with, they were pits, not surface structures. We dug our holes in the shifting dirt, then acquired planks or shiplap from somewhere for a roof, then did the best we could to lay the crumbling sod on top of the boards, complete with cactuses. The idea was to make it seem as if there were no pit there. Usually we had two crawly holes for entrance and exit. I think that nowadays no such enterprise would be allowed because of safety "issues."

I don't remember whether we raided each other's pits, or tried to destroy them. Probably not, because the teamwork involved was more enjoyable than any hostilities. That we would come home with our hair, skin and clothing covered in dirt didn't mean all that much. We were boys. I never knew a boy without knee-scabs and dirty fingernails. When someone told me that that brush lying on the edge of your bathtub was a fingernail brush, I didn't know whether to believe it.

But one winter we had a hell of a snowfall. It was just like the snowfalls we saw in magazine pictures from back east. It got cold, too. Someone with a back porch Fahrenheit thermometer said it went to ten below. In later years I took a picture every Christmas, of my two little brothers standing on the front lawn with their Christmas presents—skates dangling from their necks, toboggans held vertical beside them, their shoes on the bare grass of December 25th. But this winter when I was ten we finally got our chance to build snow forts. Instead, we got together and built a giant snowball.

Remember, we had acres and acres of snow in the boys' playground. Someone started a regular throwable snowball rolling, and it picked up snow until it was big enough to make the bottom ball of a snowman, but the boy kept going, and friends joined him, and by lunch hour the ball was a little higher than a regular ten-year-old boy. We left it outside the grade five windows for the afternoon, and when the end of school came, we raced out into the fading Okanagan sun and continued to push our snowball.

Soon it took five or six boys to push, and it was now so high that you needed to climb on top of another kid to get up there. We took turns getting to the top while that was still possible, each boy seeing whether he could remain riding while the others pushed the snowball. There were old dead cactuses and elm leaves stuck in it, along with a frozen sock and an arithmetic assignment. We pushed that thing back and forth across the boys' playground until we could hear referees' whistles being blown—time to go home. We did not think of leaving someone to guard the nine-foot snowball. That was a Friday.

Saturday morning, just before the sun struggled up over the brown hills of the Indian reserve, there were five boys pushing the snowball. There were some slight slopes in the boys' playground, but five boys could, with a lot of loud straining and some ten-year-olds' profanity, move that ball up them. When it came to a downward slope the ball would get away a little, but the snow was so deep that eventually we could run around the other side and slow it down and get it to stop. It was early morning and it was below zero in the south Okanagan, but we were sweating inside our heavy jackets. When one of us became lieutenant for a moment and declared a rest period, we willingly complied.

Let me give a sketch of the landform involved. To the immediate west of the then village of Oliver lie some brown hills that ascend to some blue mountains. At the foot of the former is a sizeable flat bench, upon which the school rests. Then there is a sudden drop to the village (now town) itself. Along the edge of this precipice runs "the ditch," a concrete irrigation canal. Near the school is a street that runs from the bench down into town. It was near that street that we stopped pushing the giant snowball late that Saturday morning.

I should mention that boys loved pushing fair-sized boulders down hillsides in those days, and I don't remember anyone getting killed down below, though I do remember parents becoming stern-faced when the discussion turned to boulder-rolling. This giant snowball perched on the edge of the drop into a snowy little town could have picked up real speed and done some real damage, especially if it followed the road right to downtown, where Highway 97 temporarily becomes Main Street. Cars could have been smashed. A house could have been demolished. A pedestrian would have been killed for sure.

But there the giant snowball perched. No one boy, no one man, could have started it rolling. It would take teamwork by a group of snowball boys, the kind that put stones in hand-sized snowballs to do that. And it never happened. That snowball stood there on the lip of mayhem while the rest of the snow in the valley melted, while all the front yard snowmen disappeared. Finally some of us made snowballs from the handy armory and enjoyed a once-in-a-lifetime spring snowball fight.

It was while the giant snowball stood sentinel on the edge of the hill just west of the house I lived in that I got a glimmer that I wanted to be someone who noticed such things and got them into something. I don't know, a poem or a story, maybe.

The Flood

Newspapers and the arrival of mail
measure my life.

The radial
influence of this mail hangup—
so that Martha, Willy, Tony, are all
hung up on receiving mail and
mail receiving competition, because
they live around me.

Ugh!
Filthy!
You smell like cheese!

Objects like that, "objects
in Garcia Lorca's poems
become aware of their relations,
start calling out to each other.

The same
happens in Picasso's work."

. . . .

What are we doing?
Poems are made by burning away
the extraneous, getting to
the fine point.

Maybe not, Pal.
. . . .

"Poems tend to magnify the emotions of their readers,
their listeners. If there is nothing there to magnify,
poetry is powerless."

!

So forget that seagull
            on thin tubular legs
standing on that rock.

                              *I swear
                              he is a hermit wizard.*

                              *That is how poesis
                              works.*

Or this, and

I sat between a man and the window that reflected his face,
my long cigarette a shadow on his image. I moved the burning
tip to the corner of his eye. He moved as if aware. I pursued his
eye with my cigarette. He became visibly uncomfortable. How
could he know? I desisted and smiled quietly. I rested in quiet
power. He was a prisoner for at least these minutes.

.

That is the way I was a captive devotee of comic books when I
was a small town lad. There were many hungers fed by the colours,
the exclamation points, the advertisements for unobtainable Yankee
items, even the staples, perfect. But the main seduction was the
scent. Today I am conscious of the attractive odours emitted by
various publishers, but no book smells as seductive as comic books
used to.

.

That's no easier to let slip than the casual part of Christmas at our

house. Bowls were put out, filled with candies, nuts, peanuts and
Japanese oranges. Someone in the family, i.e. my kid brothers, would
descend, leaving bowls of peanut shells, orange peels and the hard
candies. These objects, did they call out to each other? Or is that
not poetry?

> Maybe that is "the void profound
> Of unessential night."

> Where no man gnaws
> on another man's skull.

. . . .

I think I work otherwise.

While waiting for the mail
I stand in the kitchen, facing the spice rack.
I take the little bottles down one by one,
remove the caps, sniff.
Ah, chili powder, ah, oregano, ah, sage!
I sniff them all, providing myself
one of the induced pleasures.

. . . .

Noah: I tried to be realistic about the orders I got.

Japeth: You did the best you could. You were not trained as a ship
builder. You were not experienced in animal husbandry.

Noah: It is not easy living over time on a rocking vessel with a lot of
animals. Not easy at all. The smell for one thing.

Japeth: You did the best you knew how. As for me, I'm kind of running
out of hope. I don't think I'll live to see dry land.

Noah: [Placing his arm around his son.] Here's a reminder. Your grandfather died a week before the flood, remember?

Japeth: I know the story. The mighty Ruler whose name we must not pronounce put the flood off for a week so that we could observe the normal seven days of mourning. Yes, I remember. It wasn't that long ago.

Noah: [Sighs audibly.] Well, your grandfather lived to be 969 years of age.

Japeth: I know. That's got to be a record.

Noah: So? I don't think you have to worry about seeing dry land again.

. . . .

On the other hand
                    I know a guy so paranoid
he can't shake it,
                    wears a bullet-proof vest
all the time,
                    wears it to bed.

. . . .

                                        In poetry
                                        we call that
                                        closed form.

. . . .

2.

Picasso's christening name was

Pablo Diego José Francisco de Paula Juan Nepomuceno María de los Remedios Cipriano de la Santisima Trinidad Ruiz Picasso.

§

I was in the dark barracks room for four, having come in late, the other three airmen asleep. I was bent over in front of my locker, taking off my socks, my eyes getting used to the faint night sky's light entering the room. I straightened, and right in front of me was a face in my mirror. What a look of disgusting fear and surprise there!

§

Abraham: Some of my best friends are Canaanites, but I wouldn't want my son to marry one.

Isaac: You are so square, Dad. Square as cake.

Abraham: I have sent away for a relative of ours. She is white. She comes with money.

Isaac: I will be in my bed. I can not walk in this world with my mother gone.

Abraham: You will be comforted when this woman comes to your tent.

Isaac: I know what to expect, what a bespectacled therapist called "The dollars of reality."

. . . .

"When this Verse was first dictated to me, I consider'd a Monotonous Cadence, like that used by Milton and Shakespeare and all writers of English Blank Verse, derived from the modern bondage of Rhyming, to be a necessary and indispensible part of Verse. But I soon found that in the mouth of a true Orator such monotony was not only awkward, but as much a bondage as rhyme itself."

. . . .

I had an aunt who would look at
the bottom of every dish she used
to see whether it said China there.
She wouldn't use dishes from China.
She was afraid the Red Chinese were
putting a brain poison in their dishes
for export to America. She wasn't
going to be a casualty.

I like driving to school in the morning,
        watching the dry snow
            blowing off
                    the hood of my car.

"When the lamp is shattered."

.

Down on low class 1964 Jewish East 8th Avenue Calgary, stores full of old lampshades and 1930s console radios, there is one store where an old man, huge, with big warty bulb nose stands year after year in doorway of shop, how does he pay for it—no paint, he don't want to wipe the dust away, across the street the place run by Harpo Marx and his son who knows the old man can't sell anything, I was in there today and he was watching his father old Romanian Harpo talking to this farm woman who says "I guess I'm just too Scotch" while outside a well-dressed young Jewish guy, slick black hair neatly cut at back of his neck, there's a smooth black fur also on the collar of his cool gray grey car coat, is peering into window at second-hand quality shoes, his hands in his pockets—meanwhile old Harpo is holding a dusty saucer in his hands, clumsy and gentle hands don't know what they're doing, but I see, he's wiping the dust off the saucer, and puts cracked blunt fingernail horn in chip on edge of saucer, saying something evasive about getting a glazier to smooth it off, and she says, "But I couldn't serve it to visitors"—and I go back to my parked car on the corner, leaving image of hanging leather saddles and five-string guitars, and the rush hour traffic chases me home.

.

I had an uncle who lost
more and more control
of his body the more
scare stories he heard
about Commies behind
the bushes. A few times
I helped carry him from
chair to chair.

{83}

"What have we to do with national prejudices?
They are the inveterate diseases of old countries,
contracted in rude and ignorant ages, when nations
knew but little of each other, and looked beyond
their own boundaries with distrust and hostility.
We, on the contrary, have sprung into national
existence in an enlightened and philosophic age,
when the different parts of the habitable world
and the various branches of the human family
have been indefatigably studied and made known
to each other; and we forego the advantages of
our birth if we do not shake off the national
prejudices as we would the local superstitions
of the old world." [1819]

. . . .

You do know that Iago
sees deeply into human nature,

practices great ingenuity
in handling an intricate plot ,

and brings before our eyes
the fall of a great man.

You see that Iago is

a self-portrait of the playwright
we all love.

◆

I've noticed this
wherever I go—
even I used to do it—
though at times
I would shift,
and in my best times
shifted slightly
every time, though I
stayed usually
in the same portion
of the room, always
at the back.

. . . .

While noisily running water in the bathtub
I always think that through the noise
I can hear her shouting for me
from another room.

"Tu as l'odeur de fromage," she shouts.

—

Me, a married man—I can't really
imagine how to lie on my wife
and fuck her—I know I do, but I
can't actually imagine it—I can only
do it—it is the only thing
I can't imagine.

*

Here is something I can imagine, or have imagined long ago:

The police can use ballistic tests on turds to identify suspects.

They feed them specific foods, then collect their turds.

Suspects attempt many ruses, but the police labs stay ahead of them.

**

That is pretty darn prose-like, isn't it? Try this: our season is the sea's son,
natural progeny of the strength of the tide, the moan of its mother, was
that the moon his mother, its measure of his life.

When I was a kid the school lavatory paper towels said (it went with the
strong smell of the green liquid soap and the scary toilet doors a person
could see over or under) WIPE, don't blot. So I thought I guess the bad
boys blotted, the school was down on this—the same boys that smoked
and talked dirty about late night happenings—I didn't know whether it
was because blotting used more towels—I always connected it with my
family's thrift, and the piles of towels cascading out of and around the bin,
or some more morally determined reason.

♪

[In case you are thinking too melodically of all this,
I should inform you that my mind flicks things out
like hard balls of snot off a fingernail.]   {simile

. . . .

"More like a floating barn
than any cheese,
I'd say."

ALL TRAGEDY, EVEN ARISTOTELIAN
AND SHAKESPEAREAN TRAGEDY, IS
UNIVERSAL AND EXISTENTIAL—BECAUSE
TRAGEDY INVOLVES THE IRONIC AND FATEFUL FACT THAT
NO HUMAN CAN BE PERFECT. THE ONLY WAY OTHELLO OR
ANTONY COULD HAVE ESCAPED HIS FATE WOULD HAVE BEEN
TO LIVE WITHOUT FAULT—A CONDITION NOT ALLOWED BY
THE UNIVERSE IN WHICH CONFLICTING FORCES ARE EVER IN
MOTION.

Hmm.

"You all know that security
Is mortal's chiefest enemy."
            Macbeth III, v, 33-34.

Thinking about the horror
        of a burst blood vessel inside the cranium,
                I came this close to bursting one.

Then attained a measure of freedom because
        "Good art weathers the ages because once in so often
a man of intelligence commands the mass to adore it. His
contemporaries call him a nuisance, their children follow his
instructions, and include him in the curricula."

_____

Universal and existential. It struck me odd to be going around
Cuernavaca, saying look at the retired Americans, odd creatures,
all the *norteamericanos* I have seen have been walking around
with grim expressions—I haven't seen one with a smile—they
look as if they are doing a duty they wish was over.

It is easy to pick out the retired Americans—they are the ones
with white skin and no moustaches, except for some of the women.

They are stepping into the dark of the Piggly Wiggly store.

Ah epazote, ah achiote, ah chaya.

.

Look. When they can no longer walk

they pick up a stick
and keep moving

but when I am going down

in an elevator I always flex my knees

just in case.

.

                        Did they ever worship fire?
                        Did they fear the sun and
                        did they light an eternal flame
                        over a buried president?

A few hundred years from now
people will look at four faces
on a mountain's height
and they will not recognize them.

But when they pick up deer teeth
from the forest floor, they will know
they are stone.

        What are we doing?
            Sculptures are made by cutting away
            the extraneous, getting to
            the wide awake point.

❖

Yet where we live
  most married couples
      don't know who
          made their wedding rings.

And by the same token I feel a little threatened when I go to some do
and a strange smiling young woman inside the doorway is engaged in
putting name tags on the chests of all the people who arrive.

But hooray!
Back home the cats keep
shitting in the bathtub.

And we sleep in late every day.

. . . .

More about snow:

   A little while after we get to Toronto, the snow falls in large flakes
such as we had not seen for years except in movies about no longer
agonizing Christmas, seven fluffy inches in a few hours, the streets we drive
along through are soft with batter-brown snow—in the morning we look
out a third story window of this old house on Keewatin Avenue and see the
bare deciduous trees, the top half of each branch covered high with snow,
the air is still and FM music of strings on the radio, this is Toronto—the
heavy peace of a big city that knows it will not be moved with the wind,
and here is the corny part: a man could feel that way here too.

. . . .
[Discontinuity warning]

→   The interviewer from *Newsweek*
                                       asked C.P. Snow: "What generally
                                       does your particular job in the
                                       government entail?

Usually when your cat jumps
down from the edge of the bathtub
he makes a throaty meow sound
as his feet hit the floor.

You like him for that.

. . . .

If you would just as soon not read nasty things for personal
or political reasons, don't read this small paragraph in a box:

I often used to think about that strange country called
Dixie and how utterly incomprehensible it could be.
Take those descendants of slave-holders who could
not shake their fear of black men. I used to think
about the lynchings that still occurred when I was
a child. One would see photographs of a cluster of
homely white people, including children, around
and beneath the hanging body of a lynched Negro. I
would read that a gang of white men had cut off his
genitals before or after hanging him. I would think
of some white left hand grabbing those genitals for
the moment before cutting them off. What was that
about, I wondered, but I was just a child.

It makes you realize, such a thing, that either (a) God didn't have to
bother causing a flood, or (b) that no number of floods or fires would
teach these assholes anything.

. . . .

When they promised television I thought that their cameras
would be the extension of my eyes, to see everywhere in the world.

But when television had been here for a while I began to suspect
that my eyes and me had been annexed by their cameras.

.

Later I found out that if I really wanted to see those giant
        Egyptians
I would have to go to Egypt and look.

. . . .

It was so cold that night, so
cold in that old church we spent our nights in,
so cold we had to keep our fire alive
with whatever we could find, wood

that smelled beautiful when we
got it going, keeping ourselves warm
with relics that stubbornly caught small flames
then turned to aromatic ash

that in the light of day were cold
and in the breeze of the open door, impermanent.

_____

Somewhere around here
        there should be a lonely soldier flute
                in the middle of a vast darkened plain—

                                        In poetry
                                        we call that
                                        open form.

We ask our haystack brethren
how come God has to break his laws
to persuade his creatures
of those laws his creature
is part of?

Just askin'.

He will always say "Love,"
and we'll always say, "Ah!"

Speaker of the House: The House recognizes the Member from Bogus
River.

Member from Bogus River: "Thank you, Mr. Speaker. My question is to
the Minister for Recreation and Hobbies.

[A muffled crash is heard.]

What I would like to know, Honourable
Minister, is this. Given that our nation's National Hobby is
electric model trains—

Minister for Recreation and Hobbies: The trains need not be electric.
The National Hobby includes those few wind-up train sets that
may still be purchased in such shall-we-say less favoured regions
as Bogus River.

[Louder crash, as of bricks falling to the floor in another room.]

Member: As I recall, the Honourable Minister's riding includes Radish Prairie, a spot on our National Map that has never seen any kind of train, not to mention airplanes or taxicabs.

Minister: At least we know how to wear our trousers frontward. Will the Honourable Member get to the—

[Really loud series of crashes. A stained glass window shatters.]

Member: Why, you—

[The chamber is filled with dust as more windows shatter.]

Speaker: Will Honourable members please—

❖   ❖   ❖

"And be not conformed to this world,
      but be ye transformed
by the renewing of your mind."
                    —*Romans* 12:3

Well, I am the kind of person—when I start running the bathtub water I think someone's calling me from another room, so I turn off the taps to listen.

"I mean here that imagination is more
a power to take in and hold than
it is a power of making-up."
              —Robin Blaser, "The Fire."

When the telephone rings in the kitchen and someone
answers it I turn the TV sound off and listen, in case
it's about my mother.

....

But here is young Shelley, reporting a psychotropic day:

We lived a day as we were wont to live,
    But Nature had a robe of glory on,
And the bright air o'er every shape did weave
    Intenser hues, so that the herbless stone,
    The leafless bough among the leaves alone,
Had being clearer than its own could be,
    And Cythna's pure and radiant self was shown,
In this strange vision, so divine to me,
That, if I loved before, now love was agony.

              —*The Revolt of Islam*, III,iii.

He made some of us hear a perpetual orphic song.
Before that I slouched, pouted, pretended to be unknowable.
He made me enjoy standing straight and tall.

Standing straight and tall you can see over everything.
You can see a big smoky sign that says "The End."
That's where the quietest music is coming from.

>

Even the "Elgin" marbles, even the Caryatids
emerged when dross was cut away. That is how
poesis works.

So when Venetians blew up the Turkish ammunition magazine
September 26, 1687, the ceiling and walls disappeared
from the Parthenon.

That was poesis.

When the English hauled the marbles away,
half to London, half to the ocean's floor,
that was not.

. . . .

                        Stop for a minute,
                        recall sad 4:00 a.m. light
                        in window of grade school

                        where lone janitor's
                        sweeping, looking at floor
                        in front of him.

"Poets" get fixations
& think they have themes.

Poets tip their heads
for music. Their feet
a rhythm section.

They walk around the house
before thinking to enter.

A "Poem" wants to represent
life, express nature.

A poem is its double.

Things were kind of slow
so my uncle Ira
took a job as a Negro.

The pay was not good,
the working conditions
could have been a lot better.

"The past is of cultural interest only when it is still the present or may yet
become the future."
                                    —Edward Sapir

Their flag they display everywhere?
It has white and red stripes.
For the white people
and the blood of the others.

How did we get here
from up there?

     When I was a lad
     I saw a pile of wanted posters on a Mountie's desk.

     85% of the faces were dark.

Cases to be solved.
Races to be sorted out.
Chases to be left to the movies.

  .

[Would you believe it? I just realized that I have been talking about poetry
all this time, about how you make poetry. About what it's for, and now I
just realized that what I am saying right now is prose, and you'd think it
would be impossible to explain anything about poetry that way.]

[Those giant Egyptians knew this many centuries ago.]

On the other hand: *In the Ball State University Forum* of Winter 1970,
a professor by the name of Wm. Sutton writes seriously, with copious
footnotes, about Robert Frost's opinion of Carl Sandburg's haircut.

.

But remember, whether
you show it or
not, the quality of mercy
is not strange.

Tenderness is almost
sadness, a forehead
touched by another forehead
begins a nation.

Ω

Sunday, while driving past some retirement apartments,
I saw two old women in full Salvation Army outfits
getting into a Volkswagen with a big bumper sticker:
             HELL'S GATE

This apparition a stone's throw from the old folks'
recreation centre with the block-long sign:
TERMINAL CITY LAWN BOWLING CLUB

* * *

Ah, fuller's earth,

        ah, Stoddart solvent,

                ah, carbon tet.

We always told people we poured it through
a loaf of bread and drank it,

thrilling the rookies, keeping
our noses clean.

Knowing about mud
on the nuns' hems.

* * *

"University professors will always welcome poets who think and write
like university professors before they will welcome any poet who thinks
and writes like a poet."

On a similar note, "Nothing gathers and shows dust as much as a black
pebbly-covered Bible."

On another similar note. "A writer without theory or method is just a
momentary nuisance."

If you hear a guy on the radio saying the word "beautiful"—
look out.

He's trying
to sell you something.

Anyone knows
beauty is beyond
the reach of words,

A vision refutes words,
eradicates them. A romantic
rebels against the Word.

Religious preachers
claim we know
everything, but poetry

though left in the
body of words
will tell us

most of what there is to know
we don't know yet,
romantic poets

thwart themselves, hang
on the cross
made of words, look

or try to see
beyond the ocean
where nothing is

and awaits us.

Air Camera

In the RCAF, according to my trade training, I was an aerial photographer. Earlier, at basic training I once caught hell from my physical training corporal for having a pink tee shirt. Its colour was a result of my having washed a red shirt with my white tee shirt, and it became the earliest entry in my three year record of uniform shortcomings. I could write a book about them.

At trade training I was eighteen years old, and able to make calculations that would simply baffle me now. Not for the first time: I would now also be totally lost at the grade ten algebra I once whizzed through. But when I was eighteen I calibrated a camera the size of a washing machine inside the fuselage of a DC3 flying over Lake Simcoe and its surrounding counties. I had to calculate the plane's airspeed, its drift, its yaw, and its altitude, as well as the usual settings of the camera—focus and so on—not to mention as well the speed of the 5-inch film as it scrolled behind the open lens of the miraculous machine under my control. Or, on another assignment, setting the shutter speed and f-stop for a series of 5x8 stills. The plane flew east, then turned and flew west, just a tad north of its eastward flight. And so on.

This was the first step in making an aerial map. Back at Camp Borden I would spend a few hours developing the aerial photographs, then standing over a table while I tore and spliced the uneven edges of my wet photos, assembling my black and white map. The sadistic sergeant who assigned us our areas had made sure that mine was largely made up of featureless Lake Simcoe. I was afraid of messing up, of course, but I was also in an addlepated way having fun.

I finished at the top of my class, so I got first pick of air stations, except for the married guy with a family. He took Comox on Vancouver Island. I could have taken one in the Maritimes that spends part of the winter in the Caribbean. But I was a going-on-nineteen dolt, and took the farthest west station available—Macdonald, Manitoba. I arrived there in a snowstorm and stayed for three winters, taking the bus seventeen miles to Portage la Prairie most weekends. The land was flat and usually white.

Macdonald was a NATO air gunnery training station, so we aerial photographers spent most of our time servicing T33 jets with 16 millimetre film in gun sight and wing cameras. It was more boring than photographing caribou herds in the Arctic or beaches in Jamaica, but safer. I mention safety because there were always some prangs on NATO training stations, "prang" being a quaint service word for plane crash.

A prang provided some variety in a young photographer's life, a respite from the collecting and developing of little movies showing how well a young NATO pilot could shoot machine gun bullets through a large piece of canvas towed behind a plane in the sky over Lake Manitoba. Fatalities in RCAF planes were expected, built into schedules and plans. My friend Fred started his air force career as a student pilot. He told me that one of the first speeches he heard from an NCO informed a hundred young listeners that three of them would get their wings and three of them would be dead.

The prang I am going to refer to involved a French gunnery student who had panicked and released his canopy lock. When his instructor told him to relock the canopy so that his expulsion seat could operate, the young French pilot panicked even more and rode his T33 right into the Manitoba ground. The aerial photographs I made showed that the engine of his kite made a straight swatch through some young trees while the airframe veered to the right, creating something between a vee and a right angle.

I shot those pictures with the wrong camera, and here's why. There was a big rush on cameras and cameramen that day. Some of the latter had jumped into a truck and headed for the crash site, about twenty miles northwest of the base. I don't know where the others had gone, but some of them had taken all our aerial cameras. The photo section was bossed by a sergeant named Armitage, and he was among the missing, along with both our corporals. All at once I, a less-than-shiny leading aircraftsman (equivalent of a PFC), had the superior rank in this outfit. Ridiculous. I hadn't even got around to sewing the propellers on my sleeves.

So when the call came to get over to the tarmac, I grabbed a Speed Graphic, a knapsack full of 4x5 film holders, and a knapsack of flashbulbs. You remember the Speed Graphic; it was that camera you saw 1940s newspaper guys aiming at boxers in the ring. You should know that the Speed Graphic was not known for its speed. For every shot, even if you weren't using those big flash bulbs, you had to slide out and slide in the film sheet holder, focus the lens, and cock the shutter. Then you aimed and pressed the shutter and started again. But if you did everything right you got a nice sharp four-inch-by-five-inch negative with resolution to die for.

I didn't give a lot of thought to dying for anything when I climbed into the Expeditor. In case you don't remember, the Beechcraft Expeditor was an eight-seater with two propellers and two tailfins. This one would contain a single pilot and a single LAC photographer with a Speed Graphic. Usually when I got a ride in an Expeditor some guy would fit me with a parachute. Not this time. Instead, I got a headset, so the pilot and I could send instructions to each other. It was my job to take pictures of the prang site from above—an uncomplicated job if you have a proper aerial camera, even a K17. But with a press camera, I had to be inventive. I should have been scared out of my wits, but I was too busy.

Did I mention that I had instructed the ground crew to remove the door? Well, not exactly. With a DC3 you had to remove the whole door. With an Expeditor, you just took away the top half—sort of like Dutch doors. I was supposed to attach a cable to myself and the plane, but I was busy, and, you might say, winging it. I just hoped that when I stuck that camera out the door the wind wouldn't take it out of my hands.

Get lower, I kept telling the pilot, and bank to the left, I mean portside. I was using a press camera, after all. I needed detail. I think we got it down to four hundred feet. The Expeditor was complaining. I saw guys on the ground waving us away. I loaded and reloaded film while my body was pressed hard against the half door. I remember wondering how well it was latched.

An hour later I was in the darkroom. Not once did I feel like puking. I was working. That night while I tried to get to sleep in the barracks I thought I would get serious and start saving the poems I wrote.

May 22, 1986

We were in Geelong,
eating fruit we didn't know the name of,

my friend named Bob Kroetsch,
who belonged to another climate,

and I. I walked to the metal
waterfront of Geelong with Bob

because I was determined
to find wisdom in the Antipodes.

I mean from any source. And
it came to pass. It did.

At one point I looked down
at the strange expiring ground

and "I'm dying," I said. "It wouldn't,"
said Kroetsch, "be the first time."

A Little Montreal Sonnet

The night of Saturday
March 16, 1968

I kissed a movie star
and danced with

a federal
cabinet minister's wife.

Quite
a difference.

1985: Berlin TV

Berlin TV

Heinz loaned him an old black & white set.
Just now he turned it on. On West Berlin TV there's
a movie about a model who takes her clothes off.
On East Berlin TV they show you how to
change your tires to conserve energy.

Berlin Food

He walked seventeen kilometers in West Berlin.
Thank goodness he was wearing his old sneakers
that have been all across Canada, the western U.S.,
Mexico City, Hawaii, New Zealand, Australia,
Italy, and the bottom of Robin Blaser's basement steps.
On the way he stopped for his first German meal––
a Hawaiian ham steak.

Shakespeare's Birthday in Berlin

He went to hear Nikki Giovanni read her poems
at Amerika Haus. Her poems are not that great,
but she works the crowd well. She's a formidable
stand-up comedienne, and she knows it, her timing
works especially well if you are in front of two
in-groups, Blacks and women, and if you are
speaking, say, to a German audience. He liked her
a lot.

Dinner at Home

While it rains a North Sea on the green city all day
he decides to watch the ice hockey between Canada
and the Soviets, but first a little early supper,
European wieners, boiled eggs, little tomatoes,

cheese, an apple from Italy. There is hockey in Prague
so what are the Japanese downstairs yelling about?

Death in Berlin
Forty years ago tonight Hitler offed himself
in his bunker somewhere under here. So he
went out and bought a copy of *Stars & Stripes*,
for history, for newsprint, for a different insanity
while the spaghetti bubbled. His family didn't write,
and the communists were cursing the wet weather.

A Telephone Call from Vancouver
At 2:37 a.m., she said,
his face was staring in her bedroom window,
with full beard and anguish in the eyes
and some sort of physical and spiritual wounds, but
think of the time zone difference, think of the
brain in the dark, light along the Berlin Wall.

East Berlin TV, Black and White
Labour Day in DDR, march music, children on father's
shoulders, posters, slogans, people smiling and waving
at Honecker and friends on the reviewing platform.
Faces uplifted in joy, hands raising flowers, air cloudy
and cool, Honecker in overcoat and oldtime hat, his arm
raised for hours, must have had a prop. People carrying
flags, wait, is this communism or something earlier,
Soviet style cut-out peace doves. Microphone roars, marching crowd
roars back, programmed music, close-up cameras
getting happy faces, eyes high, this is no holiday on the calendar,
this is May Day, a nation together in its pride and beauty.
They could have been a master race.

But Then

The next day on East Berlin TV
he heard a musician explaining
the difference between jazz and funk.

So don't tell *him*
there is no progress in the arts.

"Workshop" Assignment Poem

Because I could not stop for lunch
my stomach went insane.
It gave my liver one good punch.
It squeezed my kidneys in a bunch.
I have a hunch that I should munch
my breakfast once again.

There was a lightbulb in my lunch
that lit my sandwich up a notch.
I get ideas every day
that writers in my group would botch.

There was a lightbulb up my nose
the night my brain went south.
I should have laundered all my clothes
and then dry-cleaned my mouth.

Take this little poem and run
and trade it for a breakfast bun
and trade it for a breakfast kiss
and kiss off, Miss, I'm keeping this.

A Horseradish

A horseradish
old hard but gentle root,
loud deviant bite
to wet our eyes dispute.
Past bulbous cheeks
of red runs down
one warm clear brinish blob.
Yes, wan but deep
a horseradish
to bring by night our sobs.
Mum makes our lunch
weeping with her job.
A horseradish
to bring by night our sobs.
A horseradish
to bring by night our sobs.

A Little Anthology
of Canadian Poetry
Translated into Modern English

In April of 2012 we drove back and forth across Florida for a week and a half, going to baseball games every night. Then we trudged onto a cruise ship in Fort Lauderdale, and sailed for Vancouver via the Panama Canal. This meant that despite the wonders of the electronic world, we had to haul a suitcase full of books with us. I like to read books and then leave them in cruise ships or hotels. The heaviest book I took this time was *An Anthology of Canadian Literature* (Third Edition) edited by Donna Bennett and Russell Brown (don't you love all those double consonants?) published by Oxford University Press.

Not only did I get to reread a lot of neat poetry and fiction, but I also found a project. Why don't I, I asked myself, while refusing to even consider accepting an ice cream cone, try my hand at translating some of these classic Canadian poems? After all, I had translated a collection of Guillevic's poems on a previous cruise. Besides, the activity would make me look more refined than all those other people in the ship's library, those jigsaw puzzle doers, those cell-phone jabbers.

As Richard Bentley the great 18th century classics scholar said, "A very pretty poem, Mr. Pope, but it's not Homer." That principle, I suppose, holds true here. Lucky you, Mr. Layton.

(from) The Dusty Village

You goofy sidekick of my early times,
Smiling abettor of all my boyish crimes,
With whom I rehearsed our brilliant routines,
And taught to roll the bottoms of his jeans;
Whose fine example urges patient cheer
And places no true limit on our beer;
Say if you will in this our doting age
What you might think of my poor hopeful page,
Can you forgive the errors of my pen,
And let me pat your balding pate again?
There is no gink that I could better choose
To dodge my offer to become my muse.

Translation of "The Rising Village"
by Oliver Goldsmith

(from) Sonnets Written in a
West Point Grey Lane

The trucks are grinding thoroughly, and there
    A back yard squirrel knocks the birdbath down,
    And looks at me as if I were a dolt.
    The normal spider's web enwraps my face,
    Disproving labour's dignity and care.
    I'd like to clean my face off, like to bolt,
    But rain pelts down and floods the bloody place.
    I hear big garbage bins come crashing down,
    The music of our nearby merchants' street;
    Its harmony lends solace to my brain
    And hints of Paradise beyond the fence.
    If I could only smile away the pain
    And welcome all that noise as something sweet,
This back yard's yin and yang (and clang) might make some sense.

Translation of "Sonnets Written in the Orillia Woods"
by Charles Sangster

The Hockey Player

My bare feet squeezed inside their boots,
I'm with the crowd in tough cahoots.

The outside world is full of dinks—
Reality's inside these rinks.

The music's loud and full of drums.
While I'm not out there whacking bums.

In my spare time I tape my stick
Before I swing it at some dick.

He drops his gloves, I do the same—
At last we're at my favourite game.

The fans are spilling beer and ducking;
Their every second word is "fucking."

I'm on my ass, I've lost a tooth,
I'm in my second home, this booth.

I like my fans, they wear my shirt,
They like to see the arteries spurt.

If you don't like it, kiss my nuts—
It's Canada, you stupid putz.

We love our hockey, we're no fairies—
We freeze our assets on the prairies.

They pay me for a special skill—

I hear the crowd yell "Kill, kill, kill!"

But deep inside I feel the wish
To sit beside a creek and fish.

I wish my bloody nose was straight,
I wish I'd gone beyond grade eight.

But I have promises to keep
And Swedish guys to put to sleep.

Translation of "The Skater"
by Charles G.D. Roberts

The Dogs

There are new renters now across the lane;
    We know this for there is a brand new bark.
    We'll hear it now and also after dark,
So wintry grief is on us once again.
Oh, how I wish to give those canines pain!
    I mean the blissful owners of those curs.
    I'd like to sprinkle sand fleas on their furs,
Then stand in court and swear that I'm insane.

    From up on Twelfth, and over on the Drive
The chorus of those mutts presages Hell.
    They bark because they're glad to be alive,
But on my porch I wish them down a well.
    If these are voices celebrating Earth,
I find myself regretting my own birth.

Translation of "The Frogs" by
Archibald Lampman

The Haida Gwaii Poet

She stands before us and begins her song,
This woman who will never fade away.
An ancient story boldens her to stay,
And teach us how to right our every wrong;
Her blood is mingled with her ancient foes'
Including Ottawa and all its men.
Though they make poems every now and then
They wind up writing white men's English prose.

They said her battled nation could not thrive,
They dragged in Darwin for their social thought.
The fittest came in crowds to fill her land
And poised their pens to check off every band.
But listen to her song and quarrel not—
Unlike those wise old thinkers, she's alive.

Translation of "The Onondaga Madonna"
by Duncan Campbell Scott

The Bonehead Land

Concrete and darkened glass
resist hard rain
dumped from the grim
and smog-soiled sky;
while in the bay
long ships with deep rust
in thin acid spray
grunt
at the brownish sky;
and the green slime
reaches every way.

A house finch calls
to the void,
but the puny
yet passionate tweets
falter and stall,
then rise up weak,
and falter and stall,
in these streets—
a void
over slopping of water
on dark, stained stones.

There is no beauty
in dominance,
no resonance
of stony strand,
this smoking burg
oozes under a stripped hill
like a poisoned

and shit-covered prominence
where the oil
floods the beach and the spill
fondles the city
out of the sea.

There is a beauty
of life
broken by life
but this isn't it.

Translation of "The Lonely Land"
by A.J.M. Smith

The Walking Stick

It echoes the rockslides of the province, heard
on a small town bedroom floor in B.C.—
wooden—it nevertheless speaks nary a word
but keeps old company with a grandfather's sigh.
By its pace the morning is shuffled away,
and at its tap my mother knits her brow.
This isn't her picture of a family,
but she's now the servant of her father-in-law.

It is also the old man's prop, pair to his crutch,
the two friends in his later mortal quest,
that offer him a grasp to extend his reach,
and take their place beside him while he rests.
It's long been used to tickle grandchildren's sides,
or point at things that should be done.
The daughter-in-law is having a smoke outside,
enjoying, she tells us all, the Okanagan sun.

He told me about his own grandfather's aid
that's buried with its owner back at "home."
It had one hundred faces neatly made
as can be seen in one old tintype poem.
Years later, when I stood beside his niche
in Thatcham's crumbling churchyard, I enjoyed
a dream of disinterring the family stick,
a great-great-grandson walking undismayed.

I think I knew a symbol for the first time,
though not my mother's feeling until late.
He used that stick the way I handle rime,
but never suffered music for a mate.

A Protestant, he waited, then so he went;
his family made no speeches at his rite.
His soul may have scaled the firmament—
but his walking cane just vanished from our sight.

Translation of "The Rocking Chair"
by A.M. Klein

Pentland and the Daisy

It pokes its bright yellow eye
Toward the windshield,
Riding the brilliant Volkswagen
In its little vase;
Wherever to,
It's only a region of Oz.
It breathes, it shines,
Shakes out its parasol,
Its rustling silk;

And all the while she zips,
Ricochets about,
Hands on the wheel of this tin car:
Nor ever can she be
Confined to street
But streaks higher than any tree,
Leaps from roof to roof,
Reaches inside the wind's throat
And pulls its harmony inside out.

It's day's eye.
She is slate.
It's light to come.
She swallows lightning,
Snorts out burning chrome.

But on this road, this spinning hour
These spirits breathe together and ride:
The flower, attar of hesitation,
The composer, scourge of expectation,
Becomes a burning axe,

Too fast for mortal eyes,
Splits the sky in half.

Now she's sweet dissonance:
Now the flower opens and reaches
For the rear view mirror.

Translation of "Bartok and the Geranium"
by Dorothy Livesay

The Birth of Comedy

And I happiest when I play baseball.
        Sex, music, the odor of Malbec
        are pretty good stuff;
but a ball game beats them all to hell
        winning or losing.
In my team, nature's lovely things—
        bird, fish in bird—
        meet their devotion;
we are their poets. Let them fly,
wriggle, like a flame spun.
We are their team; as a team we run.

And I watch while the darting swallows,
        dark beyond the outfield fence
        feed on flies as do we all
or send their musical cries green
        over the park the city made
of new-mown grass to be a diamond
        for these imperfect humans,
        who, lovers of divine order,
know a god's son made this game,
yet leave their Nike feet
for the headfirst slide.

A loud infielder, often leaking blood,
        I crouch like a hairy thing
        behind the eyeglasses the liner
sometimes shatters, and crack a joke
        that baseball brains insist upon
or punish when the inning's over;
        noting how many of these

        teammates are wearing pencils
and innings unfold as stanzas do,
while someone hovering over this
smiles on a perfect double-play.

                              Translation of "The Birth of Tragedy"
                                          by Irving Layton

The Waders' Moment

No exceptions:
The waders are going to get in over their heads,
But would you believe it? Lots will say
"No problem, this ain't the deep end."
And sure enough, they're okay,
If you think a lifetime of wading is okay.
I mean if you're not into underwater travel
Where there's not a dry map in sight.
And so the blank-eyed faces of those waders
Turn this way and then the other again
And again, without a moment's fright.
Of those who fell into the deep,
Most went diving where we've never been
Into water that wrapped them,
Then became them in universal privacy,
So that we imagine ourselves elsewhere,
Not grieving them but mourning ourselves
Whom fancy cannot cheat nor even divine
Guidebook trace the nameless path
Of those imagined few who
(Tread water inside a pool of light.)

Translation of "The Swimmer's Moment"
by Margaret Avison

At the Cecil Hotel

I am writing
I am writing another goddam poem
about drinking beer
and it's clearly obvious that I'm an artist
And I figure that the bartender is an artist as well
so I show him my beer poem draft
mainly the part about the draft
he poured me that tastes a lot
like a Milton Acorn poem
But it seems that the bartender
is more into nonfiction prose
the way he turns his back
and lets out an anapestic fart
Across the semidark room
two women with large arms
and large tattoos on their arms
are drinking ale and writing poems
They pay no attention
to the two bony guys slugging each other
with grimy fists. "Pat Lane
couldn't carry Newlove's jockstrap!"
says one bony guy as he slips
in the beer and blood on the floor
and the other guy kicks him in the ear
After a while the guy picks himself up
and staggers over to his table
and sits down with a beer and a book of poems
Now the beer in my belly
is looking for a way out

but I have to pass the other bony guy
on my way to the dimly lit pisser
I can't help myself
being an artist and all
I told him "Dorothy Livesay could wipe the floor
with Newlove and Lane and Alden Nowlan!"
"Wanna come outside and say that?" he says
so I go outside and say it again
He takes a wild swing and falls down
and I sit on his head
which is face down in the parking lot
"Out here in Vancouver the poets
make love, not war!" I instruct him
He lifts his hand in a peace sign
and I let him up because I'm an artist
When we get back inside
there's a guy with a big bony nose
and a bag full of mimeographed poems
"A dollar a poem," he says
"or I will read you five pages for a beer!"
I ask him what kind of poems they are
and he says "Immutable, inscrutable, marsupial!"
I buy five of them and hand him a beer
because I've heard of this guy
He rides a bicycle all over town
and jams mimeographed poems in mail slots
He has recorded every poetry reading
ever given in this town
"Welcome to the Cecil!" he says to me
"I can tell that you are an artist
writing poems in a beer parlour—
you are contumacious, salubrious, bituminous!"

And he was out the door and off on his bike
before I could show him
my latest occasional poem
with him in it, him and beer and blood
Now I am a poet without a dime
an artist without a beer.

Translation of "At the Quinte Hotel"
by Al Purdy

Get the Poet Upstairs

Get the poet upstairs however you can,
push on the seat of his pants if necessary,
     peel his fingers away from his pen,
then frisk him for other writing utensils,
     check out his shoes and his coat
     lapel,
tell him it's time to take a rest, five
     poems a day about every stray cat
and lame dog are too many for any poet
     or reader,
advise him to close both his eyes, say omm
     and then omm, until the whole universe
     drops by,
ask him to get into his striped jammies, no slippers,
     lie down and remember yesterday's poem
     about the bum on Yonge Street,
then let it go, familiar face in a comfy world, to
     walk into the library, let it go to
     find its friends between the covers
     of the university anthology.

Translation of "Get the Poem Outdoors"
by Raymond Souster

(from) Strip Poker

I denude
this shed
of things,   a
bench,   a lawnmower,   a
spider,   two books by
Mickey Spillane.

I have dropped my
pants on the floor.

Was it really
fifty years ago?

Translation from "Naked Poems"
by Phyllis Webb

Another Canadian January Night

More rain: Commercial Drive
a canyon of wet backpacks,
tennis shoes dissolving,
cars roostertailing,
while I, hunched over, cursing,
my hair flat wet on my forehead,
am sorrowfully reminded—
we share our graves
with water, our bones float:
this is a country
where a person can drown
                    simply by standing
on a corner downtown.

Translation of "Canadian January Night"
by Alden Nowlan

Suzy

Suzy takes you down
with a step-over toe-hold
she is twice as strong as Samson
and she learned it from her father.
She will touch you with her apron
in the morning after Texas
and she'll feed you shredded carrots
that have been inside her housecoat.
But when you want to wander
from her houseboat in the harbour
she will tie your feet together
and explain that she's your mother
though you know that you're an orphan.
>   *You'd like to reason with her*
>   *and you'd like to reason hard*
>   *or you'd settle for some bingo*
>   *but she's rubbed out every letter*
>   *on your card.*

Now Layton was a landlord
when he wrote his rhyming verses
and he taught creative writing
in the universe's centre
and when he caught an inkling
that professors really liked him
he said I could be the saviour
of Canadiana culture
but too many younger poets
have now looked across the border
for an ego less inflated
and an ear that still retains a little tone
>   *You'd like to wrestle with him*
>   *and you'd like to wrestle fair*
>   *but his finger's in your eyeball*

and he's got a second mouthful
of your hair.

Now Suzy's got your wallet
and she leads you to McDonald's
she wears designer bluejeans
that she pilfered from a clothesline.
And the rain just won't stop falling
while she orders Quarter-Pounders
and she lets you say you love her
but she won't give back your money.
There are puppies on the sidewalk
there are parents in the windows
they are crying out for breakfast
they will have to do without it
while your Suzy gives them names.
> *And you want to argue with her*
> *you want to argue long*
> *but you know you'll never reach her*
> *with the honest calculation*
> *of your song.*

Translation of "Suzanne"
by Leonard Cohen

Four Little Scabs

This scab on my right knee
is emblematic of my latest fall
and she has called it feckless
correctly. This scab

on my right elbow
started the same night in Curaçao
and she has called it pathetic
correctly again. My knuckles' scabs

began with some sharp edge
at the terminus of my bloody plunge
where I gathered my expensive glasses,

my camera and what's left of my hip,
and nearly made it to another sonnet.

Translation of "Four Small Scars"
by John Newlove

This is an Old Poem About Me

It was written quite a while ago.
You might mistake it for
a few
notes: abbreviations and first thoughts
jabbed around the paper;

then, as you read
it, you see a line ending
with no discernible function: end
jambment it isn't, not
even the modern kind,
more like a thinness
reconciled, a youthful jape.

Along the way there is a trope,
and beyond that, Charles Olson.

(The poem was written
while friends were dropping acid.

I'm beside the lake, high on images
of canoes and surfacing trout.

It's hard to get it right,
young poems being what
they are, young poets too:
what with all the dangers
in nature, eh?

but if you think about it
you'll agree
it's a wonder the poem made it this far.

Translation of "This is a Photograph of Me"
by Margaret Atwood

Oh, That's How

Because I couldn't learn how
to be subtle like all those
university poets and living critters
were handy, I squashed kittens
and made women suffer
and shot deer in the gut
and ignored wailing children
and made true poetry.

Now forty years along
in my university office
I talk to creative writing
students about blood and wonder
if I'm going to get a grant
this year; they read theory
and step around beetles
they could just as easily
stomp and walk away tall.

Translation of "Because I Never Learned"
by Patrick Lane

The Peach Picker

If I were a peach picker
I would hop into your bed
and leave this day's peach fuzz
all over your sheets.

Your breasts and belly would itch;
you could never go to the supermarket
without scratching here and there
because of my job. You'd wish
complete strangers would lend you
their fingernails, the damned shower
didn't help at all.

I'd leave my orchard work
in every crease of your
glistening body, neck,
inside your elbow,
where your lucky thigh
joins the rest of you. You'd be
the peach picker's peach.

Translation of "The Cinnamon Peeler"
by Michael Ondaatje

Acknowledgements

Los Pájaros de Tenacatita was a beautiful chapbook published by Nose-in-Book, and the artful hands of Linda Crosfield in bucolic Ootsischenia.

Thanks to the editors of the following publications, and maybe some that I haven't noticed or remembered:

Event (Elizabeth Bachinsky)

Cutting out the Tongue (book for Pierre Coupey's show at The West Vancouver Museum.)

Matrix 95

The Fiddlehead 253

Six of One broadside series (Judith FitzGerald)

On Barcelona

Migratory Words

One More Once, Cue Books, North Vancouver

Open Letter

Truck

In Other Words

Canadian Poetry 72 (D.M.R. Bentley) published *"A Little Anthology of Canadian Poetry."*